Low Carb Cook and Easy Slow Cooker Recipes

Fast Crock Pot Meals for Rapid Weight Loss

Copyright © 2015 by Annette Goodman

All rights reserved. No part of this publication may be reproduced, stored in a retrieval system, or transmitted, in any form or by any means, electronic, mechanical, photocopying, recording or otherwise without the prior written permission of the author and the publishers.

All information in this book has been carefully researched and checked for factual accuracy. However, the author and publishers make no warranty, expressed or implied, that the information contained herein is appropriate for every individual, situation or purpose and assume no responsibility for errors and omission. The reader assumes the risk and full responsibility for all actions, and the author will not be held liable for any loss or damage, whether consequential, incidental, and special or otherwise that may result from the information presented in this publication.

Introduction 6

Chapter 1: What is low carb diet? Who should use it and who should not? 8

Chapter 2: Low-Carb Slow-Cooker Soups 14

1. French Onion Soup (Serves 4) 14
2. Crockpot Low Carb Spicy Chicken Soup (Serves 4) 15
3. Black Bean Soup (Serves 4) 16
4. Tomato Basil Parmesan Soup (Serves 4) 18
5. Healthy Broccoli Soup (Serves 4) 19
6. Minestrone Vegetable Soup (Serves 4) 21
7. Spicy Lentil Soup (Serves 4) 22
8. Roasted Cauliflower Soup (Serves 4) 23
9. Orange Flavoured Fish Soup (Serves 4) 24
10. Sailor's Soup (Serves 4) 26

Chapter 3: Low-Carb Crockpot Chicken recipes 27

11. Chicken and Lettuce Salad (Serves 2) 27
12. Chicken Chilli Recipe (Serves 3) 28
13. Crockpot Chicken Teriyaki (Serves 4) 29
14. Chicken Salsa (Serves 6) 31
15. Stuffed Chicken Breasts (Serves 6) 32
16. Rotisserie Chicken (Serves 4) 33
17. Thai Green Curry Chicken (Serves 3) 35

18. Chicken Tacos (Serves 8) 36

19. Glazed Chicken (Serves 6) 37

20. Chicken Chilaquiles (Serves 3) 39

21. Chicken with Red Wine (Serves 6) 40

Chapter 4: Low-carb Slow-cooker Sea-food 41

22. Shrimp Stew (Serves 4) 41

23. Crockpot Gumbo (Serves 3) 43

24. Crockpot Crab Cakes (Serves 4) 44

25. Spicy Steamed Slow Cooker Fish (Serves 4) 46

26. Slow Cooker Prawn Curry (Serves 3) 47

27. Slow Cooker Lobster Bisque (Serves 4) 49

28. Fish Fillets in Coconut Milk (Serves 5) 50

29. Lemony Fish with Asparagus (Serves 4) 52

30. Slow Cooked Fish Chowder (Serves 5) 53

31. Slow Cooked Tuna With White Beans (Serves 4) 54

Chapter 5: Low-carb slow-cooker Pork 55

32. Crockpot Pork Chops (Serves 4) 55

33. Crockpot Pork and Pineapple (Serves 5) 57

34. Crockpot Pork with Assorted Vegetables (Serves 5) 58

35. Chipotle Pork Roast (Serves 5) 59

36. Beer Pulled Pork Sandwich (Serves 5) 61

37. Spicy and Tangy Barbecue Pork (Serves 4) 62

38. Low-carb Pork Vindaloo (Serves 4) 64

39. Low-carb Creamy Crockpot Pork (Serves 4) 65

40. Crockpot Pork with Coconut and Ginger (Serves 6) 67

41. Pork Cornitas (Serves 5) 68

Chapter 6: Low-carb Slow-cooker Lamb 69

42. Lamb Kheema with Peas (Serves 4) 69

43. Lamb Momos (Serves 7) 71

44. Slow-cooked Lemony Lamb (Serves 5) 72

45. Slow Cooked Lamb with Sweet Potato (Serves 5) 74

46. Asian Slow Cooked Lamb Curry (Serves 3) 75

47. Crockpot Lamb with Onions and Herbs (Serves 4) 77

48. Lamb Leg Slow Cooked in Garlic (Serves 4) 78

49. Asian Lamb and Spinach Curry (Serves 4) 79

50. Crockpot Lamb Pasta (Serves 4) 81

Conclusion 82

Recommended Reading For You 83

About The Author 89

My Mailing list: If you would like to **receive new Kindle reads** on **weight loss, wellness, diets, recipes and healthy living** for **FREE** I invite you to my Mailing List. Whenever my new book is out, I set the free period for two days. You will get an e-mail notification and will **be the first to get the book for free** during its limited promotion.

Why would I do this when it took me countless hours to write these e-books?

First of all, that's my way of saying **"thank you"** to my new readers. Second of all – **I want to spread the word about my new books and ideas.** Mind you that **I hate spam and e-mails that come too frequently** - no worries about that.

If you think that's a good idea and are in, just follow this link:

http://eepurl.com/6elQD

Introduction

For years, I struggled with picking up the right diet for myself to shed that excess fat. More so, I struggled more with trying to stick up to a specific diet program. The reason? I am a foodie and a chef and I just couldn't stand the boring diet recipes with so many restrictions. Over a period of time, I was able to figure out a diet that works best for me. A low-carb diet was the answer to all my weight issues that I was battling since I was as a teenager. And no, this diet program does not require you to starve.

A low-carb diet gets you to live a disciplined lifestyle which helps in keeping your body fitter and leaner. Now the challenge was to be consistent with the diet program without flouting any rules. I thought this was going to be an uphill task, until I figured it doesn't have to get that overwhelming. The secret lies in experimenting with your diet food to help you stay motivated. You don't have to be a master-chef to have fun with your diet food.

If you often find yourself confused about how to whip up a yummy dish for a low-carb diet, this eBook is just the perfect thing you need right now. The recipes mentioned in this eBook are not only simple but they require every day ingredients from your kitchen. Food tastes best when you cook it with some love. Nothing can beat the mouth-watering dishes that can be cooked in a Crockpot.

Sure, a lot of people perceive slow cooking as time consuming but it's really effortless. Contrary to the regular cooking methods like pan frying or stir frying, which constantly need your attention to ensure that the food doesn't stick to the bottom of the pan or get burnt, slow cooking spares you the pain. It is a very gentle cooking technique that uses moist heat to make your food more delicious without losing out on its nutritional value.

The recipes in this eBook will come in handy when you find yourself pressed for time. There are as many as 40 different recipes that will make your life easier when you are on a low-carb diet program. While your food is getting cooked in the Crockpot, you can go catch your favourite movie or put your feet up and curl up in your bed. A low carb diet will seem so much easier to follow when you have yummy food to go with it. It will almost feel like you are having a cheat meal each day.

I strongly recommend that you continue to maintain the discipline with your food habits even after you have achieved the desired results with the low-carb diet. I also hope that this recipe book is all you will ever need to motivate yourself to go from fat to fit.

Chapter 1: What is low carb diet? Who should use it and who should not?

It's pretty easy to fall prey to the formulation "low carb." A low carb diet will certainly give you the results you have always desired and knock off those extra pounds. It will leave you feeling lighter without having to starve like most of the diets.

The alarming increase in the obesity rates around the world has compelled people to resort to different diet fads. I am calling them "fads" because most of them are a random compilation of wrong diet techniques which leads to anorexia.

An anorexic person is 10 times more likely to catch various illnesses due to their weakened immune system. A low carb diet on the other hand focuses on minimizing the intake of weight gaining carbs.

Who Should Avoid This Diet?

If you are anaemic: So, you have a low-blood count or suffer from low haemoglobin problems. In such case you should not consider getting on a low-carb diet at all. At this point of time that may not be advisable. Consult your physician after you recover and ask him if it is safe for you to go the low-carb way.

Can't live without your daily dose of carbs: If you dread giving up on your daily dose of mashed potatoes, white rice, French fries, ham burgers or your favourite bread, chances are that you will not be able to keep up with a low-carb diet, even when it's worth it.

If you are yet to recover from a serious ailment: If you have recently gone through a by-pass surgery or any other serious surgery for that matter or have suffered from a life threatening disease and not yet fully recovered, you may have to let some time go before you could take up any diet plan.

Lack of determination: It takes a lot of determination to give up on all the fattening foods included in your daily diet. The results of following a strict low-carb diet will pleasantly surprise you. But if you are not up for the challenge, do not consider taking up this diet.

Pros and Properties of Low Carb Diet

You binge less: Low-carb diet will reduce your excessive food intake. Many a time we keep gorging on our favourite desserts or other such high calorie foods without thinking how many pounds will it make you put on. If you are in the habit of going overboard with your food, low-carb diet will automatically reduce your appetite albeit in a good way.

Reduction in the level of Triglycerides in the body: Excess fat consumption or refined sugar can shoot up the Triglyceride levels in your body which are responsible for heart diseases. When you cut down on your carb intake, the triglyceride levels dip relatively, thus keeping you hale and hearty.

Reduction in blood sugar and blood pressure levels: Most carbs are a proven hurdle for your body's digestion system. The carbs approach the bloodstream and shoot up your blood sugar levels. Similarly, the diet proves to be highly effective in reducing your blood pressure levels.

Eliminates the bad cholesterol: When your doctor talks about bad cholesterol, he/she is actually referring to something called as "Low Density Lipoprotein (LDL)". At least 7 out of 10 people who suffer heart attacks have an increased level of Low Density Lipoprotein in their bodies. Low-carb diet helps break the LDL particles in the blood stream and eliminate them to a great extent.

Debunking Some Common Myths

Fibre is not essential to be in perfect health: Contrary to the popular belief that fibre is not relevant for your health, it in fact helps in turning the enzymes in the intestine into highly beneficial compounds. Consuming more fibre, especially soluble fibre can go a long way in ensuring that you lose weight quickly.

Low carb means low energy: Low carb diet advises against consuming bad carbohydrates that are present in French fries or pizzas. Regular consumption of these foods will make you lethargic while making you put on oodles of weight. When you are on a low-carb diet, you tend to eat more fibre or proteins and other nutrients which leave you feeling lighter and energetic.

Low carb diet can cause your skin to loosen up: Many people believe that their sagging skin is a result of their low-carb intake. This is merely a myth. If you are on a low-carb diet, you are not just going low on carbohydrates, but also increasing your protein intake which helps in firming up your skin. People who do not follow the low-carb diet thoroughly and do not consume the required amount of proteins; end up having sagging skin.

Low carb diet can affect your kidneys: It is a common myth that low-carb diet encourages you to consume more proteins which affects your kidneys. Whereas the fact is that this diet does not suggest you to eat proteins more than necessary and causes no harm to any of your body parts.

Low carb diet increases the risk of heart diseases: A particular study has shown that people on a low-carb diet have lesser chances of suffering from heart troubles. The amount of animal fat or protein used in low-carb diets does not cause such ailments.

Low-carb slows down the thyroid function of your body: A lot of researches claim that the reduced quantities of glucose in a low-carb diet disrupt the thyroid function. However, Dr. Stephen Phinny states that the problem lies in the restricting your calories intake instead of the glucose content, thereby causing a low-thyroid problem.

Best and Worst Food Choices You Can Make

Best Low-carb Foods

Leafy veggies: Leafy vegetables are not only rich in nutrients, but they are loaded with antioxidants which makes it even easier to lose weight. Green leafy veggies like kale, spinach, turnip greens or lettuce play an important role accomplishing your weight loss goal.

Berries: Strawberries, cranberries, blueberries and raspberries have very low sugar content. This means less empty calories and more antioxidants. You can snack on as many berries you want to satisfy your hunger pangs.

Eggs: Eggs are rich in proteins and low in carbohydrates. Eggs contain a perfect blend of amino acids that are required to build tissues in your body. They are best eaten by boiling them or pan frying them when you are on a low-carb diet.

Foods You Need to Avoid

Starchy vegetables: You need to stay away from potatoes, beet root or parsnips while on a low-carb diet. These vegetables are immensely high on carbohydrates which can lead to a major weight gain. Giving up on these veggies should be fairly easy considering the variety of low-carb alternatives that are available in the form of mushrooms, bean sprouts or cabbage.

No alcohol: Alcohol can slow down the digestion process of your body as it is always the first to get burned off, leaving very little room for the body to process solid food. Slow digestion process results in slowing down of your metabolic rate, which in-turn affects your weight-loss regime.

Grains: Grains in any form like bread, pasta or spaghetti made from all purpose flour are a complete no-no when it comes to low-carb diet. A gluten-free diet is being adapted by more and more people today as it is known to offer outstanding weight loss results.

Things to Consider Before you get Started on Low-carb Diet

I took up a low-carb diet about 5 years ago and was pleasantly surprises by its outcome. As the time passed by, I went overboard and restricted my carb intake more than the specified limit. This made me feel dizzy, fatigued and left me thirstier than ever.

In hindsight, I did make a few more errors like consuming excess protein and less fat, resorting to caffeinated drinks whenever I felt exhausted and perhaps did not maintain my water intake.

This made me realise that I need to be more careful while following the low-carb diet. I would also recommend that you get yourself checked for any other ailments before you get on this diet. If you are feeling weak and do not feel so confident about taking up this diet, wait until you are ready. The following tips will educate you more about the precautions you need to take if you are seriously thinking of going low-carb:

- Drink at least 2-3 litres of water throughout the day at regular intervals

- While you are going low on carbs, ensure that your protein intake is high

- Steer clear of caffeinate drinks and alcohol

- Do not randomly pick a low-carb diet program because you want to follow the trend. Analyse if you would be able to keep up with it.

- Stick to a reliable book or eBook that gives you extensive information about the low-carb diet rather than picking off something from the internet.

- All recipes from this book contain info on estimated nutritional value per serving.

Chapter 2: Low-Carb Slow-Cooker Soups

French Onion Soup (Serves 4)

Ingredients:

- 4 medium onions, finely chopped
- 2 tablespoons olive oil
- 1 tablespoon Worcestershire sauce
- 1 tablespoon vinegar
- One inch (2.5 cm) 3 minced garlic cloves
- 1 teaspoon brown sugar
- 1/2 teaspoon pepper
- 1/2 teaspoon salt
- 2 1/2 tablespoons cornstarch
- 13.5 fl. oz. (400 ml) natural chicken or vegetable broth
- 2 tablespoons thyme
- 1 tablespoon low fat cheese (optional)

Approx. cooking time: 2 hours

Method:

1. Mix onions, butter, Worcestershire sauce, vinegar, garlic, brown sugar, salt, and pepper in a bowl and add to the Crockpot.

2. Cook it on high flame for 2 hours, let the onions turn brown.

3. Later, mix some cornstarch in water and add it to the soup, followed by broth and thyme.

Serving

Some whole wheat French bread can be cubed and placed on top of the soup. Sprinkle some basil leaves.

Nutritional Value Per Serving: *Calories: 90, Carbohydrates: 10mg, Protein: 2 g, fat: 5 g*

Crockpot Low Carb Spicy Chicken Soup (Serves 4)

Ingredients:

- 13.5 fl. oz. (400 ml) natural chicken stock
- 3-4 medium sized chicken breast pieces
- 1 medium onion, chopped
- 3.5 oz. (100 g) cabbage, grated
- 6.8 oz. (200 ml) tomato puree
- 2 inch (5 cm) 1 small green chilli, finely chopped
- 6.8 fl. oz. (200 ml) salsa sauce
- 1 tablespoon onion powder
- 1 tablespoon ground cumin

- ½ teaspoon salt and pepper
- 1.7 fl. oz. (50 ml) low-fat milk (or skimmed)

Approx. cooking time: 4 hours

Method:

1. In the Crockpot, cook the chicken breasts, onion and cabbage using chicken stock for 4 hours on high flame.
2. Once cooled down, shred the chicken and put it back in the slow cooker.
3. Now add the rest of the ingredients until the soup is nice and creamy.

Serving

Top it up with mint sprigs or basil leaves.

Nutritional Value Per Serving: Calories: 227, Protein: 18 g, Carbs: 10g, Fat: 13.6 g

Black Bean Soup (Serves 4)

Ingredients:

- 7 oz. (200 g) dry black bean, soaked overnight

- 3.4 fl. oz. (100 ml) tomato puree
- 20 fl. oz. (600 ml) natural vegetable broth
- ½ teaspoon paprika powder
- 4 inch (10cm) carrot, diced
- 4 inch (10cm) celery, chopped
- 1 medium onion, finely chopped
- Half inch (~1.30 cm) 4 garlic cloves, minced
- 3.5 inch (8 cm) 2 jalapeno chillies, minced
- 3.5 oz. (100 g) dry lentils
- 2 teaspoons cumin powder
- ½ teaspoon oregano
- ½ teaspoon ground black pepper
- 1.7 oz. (50 ml) red wine vinegar
- 1 teaspoon salt

Approx. cooking time: 3.5 hours

Method:

1. Boil the beans in a Crockpot using some vegetable broth, thrice the amount of beans. Boil for about 2 hours on medium heat. Once soft remove off the flame and let it sit for 1 hour and drain.

2. Next, add all the remaining ingredients, salt, and cook for another 1.5 hours on slow heat.
3. You can also blend the soup to form a smooth paste or have the soup with whole beans.

Serving

Garnish the soup with some coriander leaves. Team it up with a loaf of whole wheat toasted garlic bread.

Nutritional Value Per Serving: *Calories: 110, Fat: 4 g, Protein: 6 g, Carbs: 17 g*

Tomato Basil Parmesan Soup (Serves 4)

Ingredients:

- 7 oz. (200 g) tomatoes, diced
- 3.5 oz. (100 g) carrots, diced
- 3.5 oz. (100 g) onions, diced
- 3.5 oz. (100 g) celery, finely chopped
- 4-5 basil leaves
- 1 teaspoon oregano powder

Approx. cooking time: 4 hours

Method:

1. Mix all the ingredients, add to the slow cooker and add salt-pepper seasoning.

2. Let it cook for 4 hours and dispose little of the stock and vegetables if needed.

3. Alternatively, you can blend the soup to form a smooth paste and serve.

   Serve hot.

Serving

Serve it in a dish along with some green salad.

Nutritional Value Per Serving: *Calories: 103, Carbs: 8 g, Protein: 8g, Fat: 6g*

Healthy Broccoli Soup (Serves 4)

Ingredients:

- 1 tablespoon low-fat butter (or olive oil)
- 3.4 fl. oz. (100 ml) skimmed milk
- 6.8 fl. oz. (200 ml) water
- 10 fl. oz. (300 ml) chicken broth
- 1/2 teaspoon salt

- 1/2 teaspoon mustard seeds, grounded
- 1/2 teaspoon pepper
- 7 oz. (100 g) broccoli florets
- 1 finely green, yellow or red bell pepper, chopped
- 2 tablespoons chives, finely chopped

Approx. cooking time: 2 hours

Method:

1. In a skillet, warm the butter and add cream, water, broth, salt, mustard and pepper.
2. Once it simmers add all the remaining ingredients and cook for 2 hours on low heat.

Serving

Add some dried parsley for garnish.

Nutritional Value Per Serving: *Calories: 90, Carbs: 14 g, Protein: 3 g, Fat: 2 g*

Minestrone Vegetable Soup (Serves 4)

Ingredients:

- 1 medium onion, diced
- One inch (2.5 cm) 3 garlic cloves, minced
- Some fresh parsley
- 3.5 oz. (100 g) celery, finely chopped
- 1 teaspoon parsley (dried)
- 3.5 oz. (200 g) broccoli florets (finely chopped)
- 7 oz. (200 g) green peas
- 7 oz. (200 g) zucchini, finely chopped
- 7 oz. (200 g) cauliflower florets, chopped
- 7 oz. (200 g) chicken, cubed
- Some fresh basil leaves
- 13.5 fl. oz. (400 ml) vegetable stock
- 1/4th teaspoon salt and pepper

Approx. cooking time: 3 hours

Method:

1. In a slow cooker, add all the above mentioned ingredients and cook the soup for 3 hours.

2. Once the vegetables are cooked, take a part of it and blend it. Mix it back to the Crockpot. The soup is ready once it thickens. Remove it from the flame and let it cool down.

Serving

Garnish with some coriander sprigs on top.

Nutritional Value Per Serving: *Calories: 50, Carbs: 20 g, Protein: 43 g, Fat: 2 g*

Spicy Lentil Soup (Serves 4)

Ingredients:

- 7 oz. (200 g) yellow lentils
- 2 tablespoon paprika powder
- 2-3 Basil leaves
- 1 green chilli, finely chopped
- One inch (2.5 cm) 3 garlic cloves, minced
- 1 tablespoon extra-virgin olive oil
- 10 fl. oz. (300 ml) natural vegetable broth or chicken stock

Approx. cooking time: 2 hours

Method:

1. Warm the oil in a slow cooker. To it, add chillies, paprika, minced garlic and let it simmer for 3-4 minutes.
2. Now, add the lentils along with some vegetable stock and let the soup cook for about 2 hours on low flame.

Serving

This soup is best served with some air fried onion rings.

***Nutritional Value Per Serving:** Calories: 199, Carbs: 31 g, Protein: 17 g, Fat: 2 g*

Roasted Cauliflower Soup (Serves 4)

Ingredients:

- 17.5 oz. (500 g) Cauliflower florets
- 2 tablespoons olive oil
- 10 fl. oz. (300 ml) natural chicken stock
- 1 medium onion, made into a fine paste
- ¾ teaspoon salt
- ½ teaspoon pepper

- One inch (2.5 cm) 2 garlic cloves, minced
- 3.4 fl. oz. (100 ml) skimmed milk
- 1 tablespoon olive oil

Method:

1. Roast the cauliflower florets over a grill.
2. In a slow cooker, sauté the garlic and onion paste in some olive oil until it turns golden brown. Now add the roasted cauliflower, salt, chicken stock and cook for 1.5 hours on low heat.
3. Next, add the skimmed milk and cook for another 30 minutes. Garnish with pepper.

Nutritional Value Per Serving: Calories: 62, Carbs: 9.5 g, Protein: 2.6 g, Fat: 2.2 g

Orange Flavoured Fish Soup (Serves 4)
Ingredients:

- 14 oz. (400 g) fish fillets
- 1 tablespoon orange juice
- 2 teaspoons orange rind
- 1 teaspoon lemon rind

- 2 tablespoons parsley, chopped
- ¾ teaspoons salt
- ½ teaspoon pepper
- 1 tablespoon olive oil
- 20 fl. oz. (600 ml) clam stock

Method:

1. Season the fish fillets with salt and pepper, set them aside for 30 minutes.
2. In a slow cooker, add the seasoned fish, followed by all the remaining ingredients and cook for 1.5 hours on low heat.

Serving:

Serve slices of orange on the sides of the dish.

Nutritional Value Per Serving: *Calories: 150, Carbs: 5 g, Protein: 3 g, Fat: 2 g*

Sailor's Soup (Serves 4)

Ingredients:

- 1/4 teaspoon dark soy sauce
- 1 teaspoon natural butter
- 3 cups water
- 3 green onions+3 red onions, finely cubed
- 8.8 oz. (250 g) raw shrimps, cleaned
- 1 can (6.5 oz., 185 g) mussels (minced) + juice
- 6 oz. (170 g) crab meat
- 2 tsp chives
- 1 teaspoon Worcestershire sauce
- 2 cloves garlic, minced
- ¼ teaspoon cayenne pepper
- 1/2 teaspoon fish seasonings
- 1/4 teaspoon pepper powder

Method:

1. Combine water, onions, Worcestershire sauce, salt and butter in a pot and boil over low heat for 15 minutes.
2. Using a sieve, remove the onions, leaving only the liquid.
3. Pour liquid into the slow cooker and add all the remaining ingredients. Stir thoroughly. Cook for 2 hours on low heat.

Serving:

Serve with dark soy sauce and a few drops of sesame oil. This soup also goes great with dried tomatoes.

Nutritional Value Per Serving: *Calories: 138, Carbs: 6.1 g, Protein: 23.8 g, Fat: 2.2 g*

Chapter 3: Low-Carb Crockpot Chicken recipes

Chicken and Lettuce Salad (Serves 2)

Ingredients:

- 7 oz. (200 g) shredded chicken
- 1 tablespoon olive oil
- 3.5 oz. (100 g) lettuce leaves, roughly chopped
- 1 teaspoon lemon juice
- ½ teaspoon salt
- ½ teaspoon pepper powder
- 6.8 fl. oz. (200 ml) natural chicken broth

Approx. cooking time: 1 hour

Method:

1. In a Crockpot, warm the chicken broth for about 2 minutes. Add the chicken, salt, pepper powder, lemon juice and cook for 1 hour.

2. In a sauce pan, fry the lettuce leaves in olive oil, add pepper. Sprinkle the lettuce leaves on top of the chicken and mix well.

Serving

This dish is mainly served as salad.

Nutritional Value Per Serving: Calories: 340, Carbs: 13.7 g, Protein: 29.5, Fat: 19.8 g

Chicken Chilli Recipe (Serves 3)

Ingredients:

- 7 oz. (200 g) chicken sausage (diced)
- 7 oz. (200 g) pasta sauce
- 7 oz. (200 g) chopped tomatoes
- 1 onion, finely chopped
- 7 oz. (200 g) black beans drained
- 1 teaspoon paprika powder
- 1/8 teaspoon pepper

- ½ teaspoon salt
- 5 fl. oz. (150 ml) chicken stock
- 1 tablespoon olive oil

Approx. cooking time: 6 hours

Method:

1. Sauté the sausage in a pan over low flame in the oil. Add the chopped onion to the pan. Add the pasta sauce along with some chicken stock. Sprinkle some pepper, paprika powder and salt.
2. Add the left over ingredients to the slow cooker and stir. Cook for 6 hours and serve.

Serving

Serve hot with green salad.

Nutritional Value Per Serving: *Calories: 226, Carbs: 20 g, Protein: 20 g, Fat: 8 g*

Crockpot Chicken Teriyaki (Serves 4)

Ingredients:

- 17.5 oz. (200 g) chicken (boneless and cut into pieces)

- 1 teaspoon red chilli paste
- 1 tablespoon honey
- 1 teaspoon soy sauce
- 1 teaspoon coriander powder
- 1 tablespoon Red chilli sauce
- 2 medium onions, finely chopped
- $1/4^{th}$ teaspoon pepper powder
- 2 tablespoons extra virgin olive oil
- 3.4 fl. oz. (100 ml) natural chicken stock

Approx. cooking time: 2 hours

Method:

1. In a pan, on low flame, warm the oil; add chopped onions and sauté till light brown.
2. In a cooker, place the chicken pieces and add the rest of the above mentioned ingredients.
3. Cook the chicken for 2 hours on medium heat.

Serving

Add some chilli sauce to the dish while serving.

Nutritional Value Per Serving: *Calories: 153, Carbs: 5.5 g, Protein: 22.5 g, Fat: 4 g*

Chicken Salsa (Serves 6)

Ingredients:

- 24.5 oz. (700 g) boneless, chicken (chopped)
- 4 inch (10 cm) 2 carrots, diced
- 4 inch (10 cm) 2 celeries, chopped
- 1 medium onion, diced
- One inch (2.5 cm) 2 minced garlic cloves
- 6.8 fl. oz. (200 ml) natural chicken broth
- 1/4th teaspoon salt and pepper
- 3.4 fl. oz. (100 ml) salsa sauce

Approx. cooking time: 4 hours 15 minutes

Method:

1. Mix all the above mentioned ingredients; add them to the slow cooker along with some salt- pepper seasoning.

2. Let it cook for 4 hours and dispose off some of the chicken stock and vegetables if needed.

3. Shred the chicken. Add the sauce and butter and cook for 15 minutes more, serve hot.

Serving

This dish can be served alongside green salad.

Nutritional Value Per Serving: *Calories: 157, Carbs: 7 g, Protein: 24 g, Fat: 3 g*

Stuffed Chicken Breasts (Serves 6)

Ingredients:

- 6 slices of chicken breasts
- 7 oz. (200 g) spinach, finely chopped
- 2 roasted and sliced peppers
- 1.75 oz. (50 g) black olives
- 1 teaspoon oregano leaves
- One inch (2.5 cm) 3-4 minced garlic cloves
- 6.8 fl. oz. (200 ml) natural chicken broth
- ½ teaspoon salt and pepper

Approx. cooking time: 3-4 hours

Method:

1. Season the chicken along with salt and pepper. Slit the centre of the chicken breast; fill it with spinach, peppers, garlic and oregano.

2. In a Crockpot, place the chicken with the slit facing upwards, so that the fillings don't drop out.

3. Later, add the broth and cook for 4 hours on low flame. Do not forget to check occasionally if the chicken is being cooked well.

Serving

Garnish the chicken with some basil leaves. It can also be eaten with green salad.

Nutritional Value Per Serving: *Calories: 280, Carbs: 2 g, Protein: 23 g, Fat: 5 g*

Rotisserie Chicken (Serves 4)

Ingredients:

- 24.5 oz. (700 g) chicken, roasted and diced
- 1 teaspoon paprika powder
- 1 teaspoon salt
- ½ teaspoon pepper powder

- ½ teaspoon garlic powder
- ½ teaspoon basil leaves, dried
- ½ teaspoon oregano
- ½ teaspoon lemon juice
- 1 teaspoons lemon zest
- 6.8 fl. oz. (200 ml) natural chicken broth

Approx. cooking time: 8 hours

Method:

1. Marinate the chicken in lemon juice and spices for about 1 hour.
2. At the bottom of the slow cooker, place the small potatoes and cover with aluminium foil.
3. Throw in the lemon zest over the chicken. Mix well. Layer the chicken on top of the potatoes. Cook it on low flame for 7- 8 hours.

Serving: This dish can be eaten with cherry tomatoes and green salad. Alternatively, you can also cook it in a pre- heated oven, at 500 degrees and for 10 minutes.

Nutritional Value Per Serving: Calories: 147, Carbs: 1 g, Protein: 17 g, Fat: 8 g

Thai Green Curry Chicken (Serves 3)

Ingredients:

- 6.8 fl. oz. (200 ml) coconut milk (light)
- 2 ½ tablespoon green paste (chillies, mint and coriander)
- 2 tablespoons brown sugar
- One inch (2.5 cm) 3 garlic cloves, minced
- 4 chicken breasts, diced
- 7 oz. (200 g) chopped assorted vegetables (peas, broccoli and carrot)
- 3.5 oz. (100 g) baby corns
- 1 sliced onion
- 2 tablespoons cornstarch

Approx. cooking time: 4 hours 30 minutes

Method:

1. Mix the coconut milk, green curry paste, brown sugar and garlic in a bowl.
2. Now add chicken, veggies, baby corn and onion to the bowl. Transfer the entire mixture to the Crockpot and cook for 4 hours.

3. Later, dissolve the corn-starch to about 100 ml water, mix well.

4. Pour the cornstarch mixture over the chicken and cook for another 30 minutes until the curry thickens.

Serving

Basil leaves would serve as perfect garnish for this curry.

Nutritional Value Per Serving: Calories: 235, Carbs: 5.5 g, Protein: 45 g, Fat: 12 g

Chicken Tacos (Serves 8)

Ingredients:

- One inch (2.5 cm) 2 minced garlic cloves
- 1 tablespoon paprika powder
- 1 tablespoon chilli flakes
- 1 teaspoon salt
- 1 teaspoon black pepper
- 28 oz. (800 g) chicken breasts
- 2 onions, finely chopped
- 2 bay leaves

Approx. cooking time: 8 hours 30 minutes

Method:

1. Prepare garlic paste, add paprika, chilli flakes, salt, pepper and marinade the chicken in this paste.

2. Add the chicken along with the onions to the Crockpot and cook for 8 hours on low flame.

3. Once cooled down, shred the chicken, let it cook with the lid uncovered, for 30 minutes more and then serve.

Serving

Fill this mixture in the tacos and garnish with some lemon juice.

Nutritional Value Per Serving: Calories: 260, Carbs: 36 g, Protein: 23 g, Fat: 3 g

Glazed Chicken (Serves 6)
Ingredients:

- 21 oz. (600 g) chicken thighs
- ½ teaspoon pepper
- 1 tablespoon olive oil
- 6.8 fl. oz. (200 ml) pineapple juice

- 1 tablespoon honey or brown sugar
- 1 tablespoon light soy sauce
- 3.4. fl. oz. (100 ml) chicken stock
- 2 medium sized green onions, sliced
- 1 teaspoon salt

Method:

1. Season the chicken thighs with pepper and salt, set aside for 15 minutes.
2. Take some olive oil in a sauce pan and cook the chicken in it for 4-5 minutes until the sides turn brown.
3. Transfer the chicken to a slow cooker. Now add pineapple juice, brown sugar, soy sauce, onions, salt, pepper, chicken stock and cook for 3 hours on low heat.
4. Once cooled down, drizzle some honey on top.

Serving:

Serve alongside brown rice.

Nutritional Value Per Serving: *Calories: 300, Carbs: 33 g, Protein: 21 g, Fat: 5 g*

Chicken Chilaquiles (Serves 3)

Ingredients:

- 14 oz. (400 g) chicken breast, cut into halves
- 1 medium sized onion, chopped
- 1 medium red bell pepper and 1 yellow bell pepper, sliced
- 5 fl. oz. (150 ml) chicken broth
- One inch (2.5cm) 3 minced garlic cloves
- 7 oz. (200 g) sundried tomatoes
- Two inch (5 cm) green chilli, chopped
- ½ teaspoon salt
- ¼ teaspoon pepper
- 1 tablespoon extra-virgin olive oil or canola oil

Method:

1. In a slow cooker, sauté the onions, garlic and sliced bell peppers for 4-5 minutes.
2. Now add the chicken, followed by sundried tomatoes, chopped green chilli, pepper, salt , chicken stock and cook for 4-5 hours on low heat.

Serving:

Discard the water from the chicken pieces, place over tortilla chips. Garnish with fresh mint leaves.

Nutritional Value Per Serving: *Calories: 285, Carbs: 34 g, Protein: 13 g, Fat: 12 g*

Chicken with Red Wine (Serves 6)
Ingredients:

- 17.5 oz. (500 g) chicken, cut into cubes
- 1 medium onion, sliced
- 7 oz. (200 g) button mushrooms, chopped
- 10 fl. oz. (300 ml) natural beef stock
- 3.4 fl. oz. (100 ml) red wine
- 3.4 fl. oz. (100 ml) tomato puree, reduced
- Some chopped parsley
- 7 oz. (200 g) gravy mix
- 1 teaspoon salt and 1 bay leaf
- ½ teaspoon pepper
- 1 tablespoon olive oil

Method:

1. Sauté the onions and chicken in a slow cooker using some olive oil for 3-4 minutes. Later add sliced mushrooms, cook for another 5 minutes.
2. To this, add tomato puree, parsley, gravy mix, salt, pepper, beef stock , red wine and cook for 6 hours on high flame.

Serving:

Serve along with low-carb whole wheat noodles.

***Nutritional Value Per Serving:** Calories: 180, Carbs: 5.8 g, Protein: 21 g, Fat: 6.5 g*

Chapter 4: Low-carb Slow-cooker Sea-food

Shrimp Stew (Serves 4)
Ingredients

- 17.5 oz. (500 g) shrimp (cleaned)
- 2 tablespoons extra virgin olive oil
- 1 teaspoon lemon juice
- One inch (2.5 cm) 2 garlic cloves, minced
- Some basil
- 3.5 oz. (100 g) green bell pepper, chopped

- ½ teaspoon salt
- ½ teaspoon parsley
- ½ teaspoon oregano
- 5 medium tomatoes, finely chopped
- 33.8 fl. oz. (1 l) clam stock
- One finely chopped onion

Approx. cooking time: 8 hours

Method

1. In a slow cooker, take some olive oil, sauté the onions and garlic until they turn golden brown. Next, add the tomatoes and cook well for about 12-15 minutes.
2. Now add all the remaining ingredients except parsley, cook for 8 hours on slow heat.

Serving

Sprinkle some fresh parsley on top and serve hot.

Nutritional Value Per Serving: *Calories: 94, Carbs: 7 g, Protein: 11.5 g, Fat: 2.5 g*

Crockpot Gumbo (Serves 3)

Ingredients:

- 14 oz. (400 g) cooked shrimp
- 7 oz. (200 g) roasted chicken cubes
- 2 tablespoons tobacco sauce
- 1 tablespoon onion powder
- 1 teaspoon garlic powder
- 1/2 teaspoon salt
- ½ teaspoon pepper
- 7 oz. (200 g) mushrooms
- 2 bell peppers yellow and red bell peppers, diced
- 3.4 fl. oz. (100 ml) skimmed milk
- 3.4 fl. oz. (100 ml) clam stock

Approx. cooking time: 8 hours

Method:

1. In a slow cooker, throw in all the above mentioned ingredients leaving shrimp and chicken. Let this mixture cook for Approx. 3-3.5 hours on high flame.

2. The next step is to shred the chicken and add it to the slow cooker, followed by shrimp.

3. Cook for another 1 hour on high. Serve hot.

Serving

You can eat this dish with some cooked whole wheat noodles.

Nutritional Value Per Serving: *Calories: 257, Carbs: 35 g, Protein: 28 g, Fat: 1 g*

Crockpot Crab Cakes (Serves 4)
Ingredients:

- 17.5 oz. (500 g) crab meat
- 1.7. fl. oz. (50 ml) clam or shrimp stock
- 2 teaspoons onion powder
- 1 red bell pepper, finely chopped
- 3/4th teaspoon garlic powder
- ½ teaspoon pepper
- 1 tablespoon olive oil
- 1 tablespoon lemon juice
- ½ teaspoon salt
- 7 oz. (200 g) bread crumbs
- 1 egg (beaten)

Method:

1. In a slow cooker, sauté the bell pepper using some olive oil for about 8-9 minutes.

2. Now add all the ingredients mentioned above except the last two (bread crumbs and egg) and let the crab mixture cook for 45 minutes on slow heat.

3. Once cooled down, make small circular cakes using your hands. Dip them in the egg, coat them with bread crumbs and shallow fry them over slight olive oil in a pan.

Serving

Sprinkle some coriander leaves while serving the crab cakes.

Nutritional Value Per Serving: *Calories: 130, Carbs: 8 g, Protein: 17 g, Fat: 2.5 g*

Spicy Steamed Slow Cooker Fish (Serves 4)

Ingredients

- 28 oz. (800 g) whole fish
- 2 tablespoons lemon juice
- 2 tablespoons red chilli paste
- 1 tablespoon fish sauce
- 1 teaspoon fresh ginger paste
- ½ teaspoon turmeric powder
- 1/4th teaspoon pepper
- ½ teaspoon salt
- 2 tablespoons extra virgin olive oil

Approx. cooking time: 45 minutes

Method

1. In a bowl, mix the lemon juice, red chilli paste, fish sauce, ginger paste, pepper, turmeric powder and salt.
2. Now slit the fish and coat it with the above mixture. Set the fish aside for an hour. Lay the fish on a plate.
3. Fill the slow cooker with some hot water and set a steamer in it. Be sure that the water does not reach the steamer.

4. Now place the fish plate on top of the steamer, cover the lid and cook for 40-45 minutes on low heat. Check if the fish is done by piercing a toothpick inside it. Cook for another 10 minutes if you feel it's undercooked.

Serving: Cut a lemon slice, chop some coriander leaves and place on top of the fish when you serve them

Nutritional Value Per Serving: *Calories: 174, Carbs: 6 g, Protein: 30 g, Fat: 3 g*

Slow Cooker Prawn Curry (Serves 3)
Ingredients:

- 2 tablespoons olive oil
- 17.5 (500 g) cleaned prawns
- One inch (2.5 cm) 3 garlic cloves, minced
- 1 medium onion, finely chopped
- ½ teaspoon turmeric powder
- 1 teaspoon ginger paste
- 1 teaspoon cumin powder
- 3.4 fl. oz. (100 ml) clam stock (or shrimp stock)
- 13.5 fl. oz. (400 ml) homemade tomato puree

- 1 tablespoon lime juice
- ½ tablespoon pepper powder
- 1 teaspoon fish curry powder

Approx. cooking time: 3 hours

Method

1. In a slow cooker, take some olive oil, sauté the onions and garlic till golden brown.
2. Now add turmeric, cumin powder, pepper, tomato puree, fish curry powder, lemon juice and cook for about 1 hour.
3. Now add the prawns, cover the lid of the Crockpot and cook it for another 3 hours.

Serving

Serve this yummy curry with some chopped coriander or mint sprigs on top.

Nutritional Value Per Serving: *Calories: 84, Carbs: 0 g, Protein: 18 g, Fat: 1 g*

Slow Cooker Lobster Bisque (Serves 4)

Ingredients:

- 20.3 fl. oz. (600 ml) clam stock
- 6.8 fl. oz. (200 ml) vegetable stock
- 17.5 oz. (500 g) lobster
- 2 lobster tails
- 3.5 oz. (100 g) button mushrooms, thinly sliced
- 3.5 oz. (100 g) sundried tomatoes
- 3.4 fl. oz. (100 ml) tomato puree
- 1 teaspoon onion powder
- 1 teaspoon garlic powder
- ½ teaspoon oregano
- ½ teaspoon pepper powder
- ½ teaspoon salt

Approx. cooking time: 8 hours

Method

1. In a slow cooker, add all the above mentioned ingredients and cook for about 8 hours. Cook it on slow for the first 3 hours and later cook on low heat for another 5 hours.

2. Now using a hand blender, blend the mixture to form a chowdery broth.

3. Next, add the lobster tails and cook it for 45 minutes until the meat is tenderised.

Serve

Serve the lobster chowder in a large soup plate. If you wish, you can remove the lobster tails and use it to flavour a soup.

Nutritional Value Per Serving: *Calories: 248, Carbs: 13 g, Protein: 20 g, Fat: 12.8 g*

Fish Fillets in Coconut Milk (Serves 5)

Ingredients:

- 28 oz. (800 g) fish fillets
- 2 medium red and green bell pepper, chopped
- one inch (2.5 cm) 5 garlic cloves, minced
- 1 finely chopped onion
- 4 medium tomatoes, roughly chopped
- 10 fl. oz. (300 ml) coconut milk
- ¾th teaspoon white pepper powder

- 2 tablespoons extra virgin olive oil

Approx. cooking time: 2.5 hours

Method

1. In a slow cooker, sauté the onions and garlic slightly in olive oil for about 2-3 minutes. Now add all the remaining ingredients and slow cook for 1.5 hour.

2. Later, add the fish fillets, cover the lid of the Crockpot and cook for another 1 hour.

Serving

Serve the fish with some lemon slices on top.

***Nutritional Value Per Serving:** Calories: 370, Carbs: 7.5 g, Protein: 14.5 g, Fat: 7.7 g*

Lemony Fish with Asparagus (Serves 4)

Ingredients:

- 17.5 oz. (500 g) fish fillets
- 4 tablespoon lemon juice
- ¾ teaspoon pepper powder
- ½ teaspoon salt
- 1 tablespoon olive oil
- One inch (2.5 cm) 1 minced garlic clove
- 1 tablespoon barbecue sauce
- Four inch (10cm) 3 asparagus sticks, chopped

Method:

1. Divide aluminium foil into 8 equal parts. In a bowl, combine fish fillets with lemon juice, pepper, salt, olive oil, minced garlic and mix well.
2. Now add a bit of the fish mixture into each of these foils, wrap them. Lay them on a steamer plate and later on a trivet.
3. Take some hot water in a slow cooker and place the trivet in it. Cook the fillets for 2 hours on medium heat.

Serving:

Garnish with some lemon slices on the sides and serve hot.

Nutritional Value Per Serving: *Calories: 300, Carbs: 18 g, Protein: 25 g, Fat: 6g*

Slow Cooked Fish Chowder (Serves 5)
Ingredients:

- 17.5 oz. (500 g) fish fillets
- Approx. 5 oz. (150 g) bacon, diced
- 1 medium onion, chopped
- ½ teaspoon cayenne pepper
- ½ teaspoon salt
- Approx. 5 oz. (150 g) sweet potatoes, diced
- 4.2 fl. oz. (125 ml) skimmed milk

Method:

1. In a slow cooker, sauté the onions and bacon until it becomes golden brown. Drain the juice. Add sweet potatoes, pepper, salt and cook for 7-8 hours on low-heat.
2. Now add the skimmed milk and cook for another 60 minutes.

Serving:

Garnish with some dried parsley and serve hot

Nutritional Value Per Serving: *Calories: 125, Carbs: 28g, Protein: 4 g, Fat: 1.1 g*

Slow Cooked Tuna with White Beans (Serves 4)
Ingredients:

- 14 oz. (400 g) tuna, flaked
- One inch (2.5 cm) 1 garlic clove, minced
- 2 medium tomatoes, finely chopped
- Some basil leaves
- 3.5 oz. (100 g) white beans (soaked overnight)
- 6.8 fl. oz. (200 ml) clam stock
- ½ teaspoon pepper
- ½ teaspoon salt
- 1 teaspoon basil, dried
- ½ teaspoon ginger, shredded
- 1 tablespoon olive oil

Method:

1. In a slow cooker, sauté the garlic until turns golden brown. Now add the tomatoes and cook for 10-12 minutes.

2. Add white beans, salt, pepper, ginger, clam stock and cook for 2 hours on high.

3. Next, add the tuna and cook for 30 minutes on high.

Serving: Garnish with some lemon slices on the side.

Nutritional Value Per Serving: Calories: 249, Carbs: 21g, Protein: 17.5 g, Fat: 11 g

Chapter 5: Low-carb slow-cooker Pork

Crockpot Pork Chops (Serves 4)

Ingredients:

- 17.5 oz. (500 g) boneless pork chops
- 1 teaspoon salt
- 1 teaspoon pepper powder
- 2 medium onions, finely chopped
- ½ teaspoon thyme
- 17 fl. oz. (500 ml) chicken stock

- 1 teaspoon garlic powder
- 1 medium bell pepper, finely chopped
- 1 tablespoon lemon juice
- 1 teaspoon olive oil

Approx. cooking time: 6 hours

Method

1. Heat a sauce pan, add some olive oil and place the pork chops on it. Season with some pepper and salt and cook on high heat for about 7-8 minutes until the outer sides turn brown.
2. Spray the bottom of the slow cooker with some olive oil and add all the above mentioned ingredients. Now lay the pan fried pork chops on it.
3. Cover the lid of the cooker and cook the pork chops for 6 hours on low heat.

Serving

Serve the pork in a large dish along with some baked onion rings.

Nutritional Value Per Serving: *Calories: 260, Carbs: 5 g, Protein: 25 g, Fat: 15 g*

Crockpot Pork and Pineapple (Serves 5)

Ingredients:

- Approx. 26 oz. (750g) Pork pieces
- 14 oz. (400 g) pineapple, chopped
- 2 Green bell peppers cut into big squares
- One inch (2.5cm) 3 minced garlic cloves,
- 1.7 fl. oz. (50 ml) hoisin sauce
- 1.7 fl. oz. (50 ml) barbecue sauce
- ¾ teaspoon salt
- ½ teaspoon chilli flakes
- ½ teaspoon pepper powder
- 2 tablespoon pineapple juice

Approx. cooking time: 4 hours 30 minutes

Method

1. In a slow cooker, combine minced garlic, pork pieces, salt, pepper, hoisin sauce and pineapple juice. Cook this mixture for 4 hours on low heat.//
2. In a bowl, combine barbecue sauce, soy sauce and pour it into the cooked pork. Add the pineapple pieces, bell pepper, mix well.

3. Cover the lid of the cooker and cook for another 30 minutes.

Serving: Serve the pork, pineapple mixture along with the bell pepper pieces inserted on to wooden picks.

Nutritional Value Per Serving: Calories: 420, Carbs: 40 g, Protein: 39 g, Fat: 10 g

<u>*Crockpot Pork with Assorted Vegetables (Serves 5)*</u>
<u>Ingredients:</u>

- 14 oz. (400 g) pork chops
- 3.5 oz. (100 g) carrots, diced
- 3.5 oz. (100 g) broccoli florets
- 3.5 oz. (100 g) sweet potatoes, diced
- 3.5 oz. (100 g) zucchini, diced
- 1 onion, sliced
- Some basil leaves
- 2 tablespoons extra virgin olive oil
- 1 teaspoon garlic, minced
- ½ teaspoon pepper

- ½ teaspoon garlic salt

Approx. cooking time: 4 hours

Method

1. In a bowl, combine salt, pepper, garlic, pork and mix well. In a sauce pan, fry the pork over some olive oil on high flame for about 4-5 minutes until the outer sides turn brown.
2. Grease a slow cooker with some olive oil; add all the ingredients in it including the pork chops except the basil leaves.
3. Now cover the lid and cook the pork for 4 hours on low heat.

Serving

Serve the pork dish with basil leaves on top.

Nutritional Value Per Serving: Calories: 299, Carbs: 40 g, Protein: 28 g, Fat: 20 g

Chipotle Pork Roast (Serves 5)

Ingredients:

- 24.5 oz. (700 g) pork shoulders, sliced
- 1 teaspoon garlic powder

- 1 teaspoon onion powder

- 3.5 oz. (100 g) sweet potatoes, diced

- 1 tablespoon extra-virgin olive oil

- 6.8 fl. oz. (200 ml) salsa sauce

- 14 oz. (200 g) chipotle chiles

- 2 tablespoons corn starch

- 1 teaspoon cumin powder

- ¾ teaspoon salt

Approx. cooking time: 8 hours

Method

1. Apply some olive oil over the pork slices. In a bowl, mix the salsa sauce, chipotle, onion & garlic powder, sweet potatoes, cumin powder, salt and mix well.

2. Grease the bottom of the slow cooker with some oil. Place the pork slices on it, followed by the above mixture. Cook on low heat for 8 hours.

3. Now mix corn starch in some water, pour this liquid into the pork and cook for another 20 minutes until the dish thickens. Serve hot.

Serving

Serve this dish along with stir fried vegetables and sprinkle some coriander leaves on top as a garnish.

Nutritional Value Per Serving: *Calories: 120, Carbs: 4 g, Protein: 12 g, Fat: 6 g*

Beer Pulled Pork Sandwich (Serves 5)

Ingredients:

- Approx. 26 oz. (750 g) pork roast
- 1 teaspoon salt
- ½ teaspoon pepper powder
- 1 tablespoon onion powder
- 1 teaspoon garlic powder
- 5 fl. oz. (150 ml) beer
- 5 fl. oz. (150 ml) barbecue sauce
- Toasted whole wheat bread

Approx. cooking time: 9 hours

Method

1. In a bowl, coat the pork with salt, pepper, onion and garlic powder and mix well.

2. Grease the bottom of the slow cooker with some olive oil. Now transfer the pork onto the cooker, cover the lid and cook for 8 hours on low heat.

3. Once cooled down, shred the pork and stir in some barbecue sauce and beer. Let it cook for another 60 minutes on medium heat.

Serving

Fill this mixture inside whole wheat bread slices and serve.

Nutritional Value Per Serving: *Calories: 335, Carbs: 42 g, Protein: 21 g, Fat: 8 g*

Spicy and Tangy Barbecue Pork (Serves 4)
Ingredients

- 17.5 oz. (500 g) pork ribs
- 5 fl. oz. (150 ml) salsa sauce
- 1 tablespoon red wine vinegar
- 1 teaspoon lemon juice
- 0.3 oz. (10 ml) natural chicken stock
- 1 teaspoon Dijon mustard
- ½ teaspoon chilli flakes
- Some lemon zest

- ½ teaspoon pepper powder
- ½ teaspoon salt
- 1 teaspoon garlic powder
- ½ teaspoon paprika powder
- 1 teaspoon Worcestershire sauce

Approx. cooking time: 8 hours

Method

1. Combine salsa sauce, red wine vinegar, mustard, chilli flakes, lemon juice and zest, salt, pepper, Worcestershire sauce, garlic and paprika powder in a bowl.
2. Now place the pork ribs in a greased slow cooker. Pout the above sauce on it and cook for 8 hours on low heat.

Serving

You can sprinkle some dried oregano on top of the dish while serving.

Nutritional Value Per Serving: *Calories: 440, Carbs: 40 g, Protein: 32 g, Fat: 12 g*

Low-carb Pork Vindaloo (Serves 4)

Ingredients

- 17.5 oz. (500 g) pork steaks, sliced
- Approx. 5 oz. (150 g) sweet potato, minced
- 1 tablespoon olive oil
- Two inch (5 cm) cinnamon stick
- 1 teaspoon garlic powder
- 1 teaspoon cumin
- Half inch (2.5 cm) 2 cardamom pods
- 1 bay leaf
- 3.4. fl. oz. (100 ml) chicken broth
- 10 fl. oz. (300 ml) tomato puree
- ½ teaspoon turmeric powder
- 1 teaspoon fresh ginger paste
- 2 tablespoon apple cider vinegar
- 2 inch (5 cm) green chilli, finely chopped
- ¾ teaspoon salt

Approx. cooking time: 10 hours

Method

1. Marinate the pork slices in ginger paste and garlic powder for about 2 hours.

2. In a slow cooker, fry the bay leaf, cardamom pods and cinnamon stick in some olive oil for 3-4 minutes.

3. To this, add green chillies, sauté them and then add the tomato puree.

4. When the puree thickens a slight bit, add the rest of the ingredients along with the pork, cover the lid and let it cook for 10 hours. Cook on high heat for the first 4 hours and on low for the next 6 hours. Serve hot.

Serving

Serve in small portions along with some whole bread.

Nutritional Value Per Serving: *Calories: 161, Carbs: 10.5 g, Protein: 12 g, Fat: 8.5 g*

Low-carb Creamy Crockpot Pork (Serves 4)
Ingredients:

- 17.5 oz. (500g) pork chops
- 3 tablespoons extra virgin olive oil
- ¾ teaspoon salt
- 1 teaspoons pepper

- 2 small onions, finely chopped
- 6.8. fl. oz. (200 ml) beef stock
- 1 chicken bouillon cube
- 3.4. fl. oz. (100 ml) skimmed or low-fat milk
- one inch (2.5cm) 3 garlic cloves, minced

Method:

1. Season the pork chops with olive oil salt and pepper. Set them aside for approximately 2 hours in the refrigerator.
2. In a slow cooker, fry the onions and garlic for 7-8 minutes. Now place the pork chops over it. Mix the bullion in some hot water and pour it on top of the chops.
3. Add some beef stock and cook the pork chops for 7-8 hours over low heat.
4. Once done, add some milk and cook it again uncovered for 30 minutes.

Serving: Serve with some hot brown rice.

Nutritional Value Per Serving: *Calories: 173, Carbs: 7.5 g, Protein: 14 g, Fat: 9.5 g*

Crockpot Pork with Coconut and Ginger (Serves 6)
Ingredients:

- 17.5 oz. (500 g) pork roast, sliced
- 1 medium sized onion, made into paste
- 10 fl. oz. (300 ml) light coconut milk
- 2 teaspoon ginger (shredded)
- 1 teaspoon cumin powder
- One inch (2.5 cm) 3 minced garlic cloves
- 1 tablespoon lemon juice
- ¾ teaspoon salt
- ½ teaspoon pepper
- Two inch (5 cm) 2 slit mild green chillies
- 2 tablespoons canola oil

Method:

1. In a bowl, mix the cumin powder, salt, pepper, some oil and coat the pork roast with this seasoning.
2. Place the pork roast in a slow cooker; add ginger, garlic and onion paste. Pour the coconut milk on top.
3. Cook the pork on high for 5 hours and later on low heat for the next 9 hours until it is tenderized.

Serving: Serve with Indian whole wheat flat bread.

Nutritional Value Per Serving: Calories: 246, Carbs: 5 g, Protein: 30 g, Fat: 10 g

Pork Cornitas (Serves 5)
Ingredients:

- 21 oz. (600 g) pork butt (also called "Boston butt")
- 1 large onion, thinly sliced
- 1 tablespoon cumin powder
- 1 teaspoon thyme
- 1 tea spoon red chilli flakes
- ¾ teaspoon salt
- ½ teaspoon pepper
- One inch (2.5cm) 3 minced garlic cloves
- 10 fl. oz. (300 ml) beef stock
- 2 tablespoon extra-virgin olive oil

Method:

1. Take some olive oil in a cooker and fry the garlic until golden brown. Add chopped onion and fry again for 4-5 minutes.

2. Trim the fat of the pork, shred it.

3. Add the shredded pork into the slow cooker, followed by cumin, salt, thyme, chilli flakes, pepper, beef stock and cook for 7 hours on medium heat.

Serving:

Garnish with some chopped parsley. Serve with some wine.

Nutritional Value Per Serving: *Calories: 190, Carbs: 3 g, Protein: 27 g, Fat: 8 g*

Chapter 6: Low-carb Slow-cooker Lamb

Lamb Kheema with Peas (Serves 4)

Ingredients:

- 17.5 oz. (500 g) minced lamb
- Approx. 5 oz. (150 g) green peas
- 1 medium onion, finely chopped
- One inch (2.5 cm) 3 minced garlic cloves
- 1 teaspoon coriander powder and 1 teaspoon cumin powder
- ½ teaspoon garam masala
- 1 finely chopped mild green chili

- Some chopped mint leaves
- ½ teaspoon shredded ginger
- ¾ teaspoon salt
- 1 bay leaf
- 1 teaspoon olive oil
- 3.4 fl. oz. (100 ml) natural chicken stock
- Some cilantro leaves (for garnish)

Approx. cooking time: 2.5 hours

Method

1. Take some olive oil in a slow cooker, sauté the onions and garlic. Now add the bay leaf, shredded ginger and cook for 2-3 minutes.
2. To this, add cumin powder, garam masala, green chili, mint leaves, salt, green peas, stir well. Now add the minced lamb to this mixture along with some chicken stock and cook for 2- 2.5 hours over low heat.

Serving: Sprinkle some chopped cilantro on top.

***Nutritional Value Per Serving:** Calories: 480, Carbs: 19g, Protein: 21 g, Fat: 26 g*

Lamb Momos (Serves 7)
Ingredients (the filling):

- Approx. 12 oz. (350 g) lamb, minced
- ½ teaspoon paprika powder
- ½ teaspoon pepper
- ½ teaspoon salt
- 1 teaspoon soy sauce
- 1 teaspoon lemon juice
- 1 green chili, finely chopped
- One teaspoon oil

Ingredients (for the dough):

- 10.5 oz. (300 g) whole wheat flour
- 1/4 teaspoon salt
- some water

Approx. cooking time: 1 hour 10 minutes

Method

1. Combine all the ingredients of the filling in a bowl, fry them with some oil in a slow cooker for about 45 minutes on low heat.

2. Knead a soft dough using all the ingredients and cover it with a plastic film for about 20 minutes. Roll the dough into small circles, fill some lamb mixture, seal it. Place the momos on a dish.

3. Take some water in another slow cooker and set a steamer stand in it. Place the momos on top of the steamer and let them steam for 60-70 minutes on low heat until they are cooked properly.

Serving

Serve these momos alongside some light soy sauce.

***Nutritional Value Per Serving:** Calories: 62, Carbs: 5 g, Protein: 2 g, Fat: 1.5 g*

Slow-cooked Lemony Lamb (Serves 5)
Ingredients:

- Approx. 26 oz. (750 g) boneless lamb leg pieces
- 1 tablespoon olive oil
- ½ teaspoon salt
- ½ teaspoon pepper powder
- 2 teaspoons mixed herbs
- One inch (5cm) 3 minced garlic cloves
- 1 tablespoon lemon juice

- Some lemon zest

- 1.7 fl. oz. (50 ml) natural beef or chicken stock

- Stir fried vegetables for serving

Approx. cooking time: 3 hours

Method

1. Slit the lamb pieces with the help of a knife.
2. Take some olive oil in a saucepan and place the lamb pieces in it, sprinkle some salt and pepper. Fry the lamb on high heat until the sides turn brown.
3. Grease the slow cooker with some olive oil, place the fried lamb slices in it and throw in all the rest of the ingredients.
4. Cover the lid of the cooker and cook for 3 hours on low heat.

Serving: Serve this dish alongside some stir fry vegetables.

Nutritional Value Per Serving: *Calories: 352, Carbs: 27 g, Protein: 32 g, Fat: 9 g*

Slow Cooked Lamb with Sweet Potato (Serves 5)

Ingredients:

- Approx. 26 oz. (750 g) lamb shoulder (sliced)
- 1 medium onion, finely chopped
- 4 inch (10 cm) celery, chopped
- One inch (2.5 cm) 2 minced garlic cloves
- 3.4 fl. oz. (100 ml) reduced tomato puree
- ½ teaspoon pepper powder
- 17 fl. oz. (500 ml) chicken or beef stock
- 2 sweet potatoes (1 lbs, approx. 450 g), diced
- 10-12 spinach leaves, chopped
- ¾ teaspoon salt
- 1 tablespoon olive oil

Approx. cooking time: 3 hours

Method

1. Season the lamb pieces by sprinkling some salt and pepper on it. Fry them in a sauce pan in olive oil at high heat for 3-4 minutes until the sides turn brown.

2. Grease the slow cooker with some oil, add minced garlic, onion and fry them for a minute.

3. Now add all the remaining ingredients, followed by the fried lamb pieces and cook them for 3 hours until the lamb is tenderized.

Serving

Serve the lamb with some sliced lemon on the sides.

Nutritional Value Per Serving: Calories: 373, Carbs: 43 g, Protein: 29 g, Fat: 12 g

Asian Slow Cooked Lamb Curry (Serves 3)
Ingredients:

- 17.5 oz. (500 g) lamb shoulders, pieced
- 1 tablespoon olive oil
- 6.8 fl. oz. (200 ml) coconut milk
- one inch (2.5 cm) 2 minced garlic cloves
- 1 teaspoon freshly shredded ginger
- 1 teaspoon curry powder
- 1 medium onion, finely chopped
- 1 teaspoon mixed herbs

- 1 bay leaf
- 1 green chili, finely chopped
- ½ teaspoon salt
- 6.8 fl. oz. (200 ml) vegetable stock

Approx. cooking time: 6 hours

Method

1. In a sauce pan, take some olive oil and sauté the garlic and chopped onion for 2-3 minutes. Add green chili, bay leaf, shredded ginger, fry for another 3 minutes.

2. Now add all the remaining ingredients to the cooker along with the lamb and cook for 6 hours on low heat until the lamb is tenderized. Serve hot.

Serving

You can eat this curry along with some brown rice and garnish it with fresh coriander leaves.

Nutritional Value Per Serving: *Calories: 252, Carbs: 12 g, Protein: 14 g, Fat: 21 g*

Crockpot Lamb with Onions and Herbs (Serves 4)

Ingredients:

- 17.5 oz. (500 g) lamb, whole
- 4 large onions, thinly sliced
- ½ teaspoon thyme
- ½ teaspoon rosemary
- ½ teaspoon oregano
- ½ teaspoon parsley, dried
- ½ teaspoon pepper powder
- ¾ teaspoon salt
- 3.4 fl. oz. (100 ml) natural beef stock
- 2 tablespoons extra virgin olive oil

Method:

1. Put the lamb piece in a large bowl. Coat it with some extra virgin olive oil properly.

2. Sprinkle all the above mentioned herbs along with salt, pepper powder and mix well. Let the lamb piece marinate for 60 minutes.

3. Grease the slow cooker with some oil. Transfer the marinated lamb into it, cover the lid and cook for 6 hours on low heat.

Serving:

This dish can be eaten with some stir fried veggies on the side.

Nutritional Value Per Serving: *Calories: 394, Carbs: 8 g, Protein: 48 g, Fat: 20 g*

Lamb Leg Slow Cooked in Garlic (Serves 4)
Ingredients:

- 17.5 oz. (500 g) lamb leg
- 1 teaspoon rosemary, dried
- Handful of mint leaves, chopped
- 1 tablespoon lemon juice
- One inch (2.5 cm) 5 minced garlic cloves
- 3 tablespoons extra virgin olive oil
- ¾ teaspoon salt
- ½ teaspoon pepper
- 1 tablespoon honey (optional)

Method:

1. In a bowl, combine the lemon juice, mint leaves, chopped garlic, pepper, salt, rosemary, honey, oil and mix it well.

2. Now smear this mixture all over the lamb and let it sit for 7-8 hours in the refrigerator.

3. Take a sauce pan and cook the lamb for a few minutes on high heat until the sides turn brown.

4. Transfer the lamb to a slow cooker and let it cook for 8 hours.

Serving:

You can serve some mint sauce and wine along with this dish.

Nutritional Value Per Serving: *Calories: 487, Carbs: 13 g, Protein: 29 g, Fat: 22 g*

Asian Lamb and Spinach Curry (Serves 4)
Ingredients:

- 17.5 oz. (500 g) lamb leg, sliced into medium size pieces
- 3 medium sized onions, finely chopped
- 1 bunch of baby spinach leaves (about 20 leaves), chopped
- 1 teaspoon fresh ginger, shredded

- 2 teaspoon cumin powder
- ¾ teaspoon pepper and ¾ teaspoon salt
- 10 fl. oz. (300 ml) natural beef stock
- 3 tablespoons canola oil or extra virgin olive oil
- 2 tablespoons of low-fat yogurt

Method:

1. Fry the garlic and onions in a slow cooker using some oil.
2. When they start turning slightly brownish, add minced garlic, ginger, cumin powder, pepper and fry for another 5-7 minutes. Now pour the stock and cook on high heat for 10 minutes.
3. Now add the lamb pieces and cook for 8 hours on low heat. Once cooled down, add chopped spinach and cook for another 10-15 minutes. Add two tablespoon of low-fat yogurt, stir and serve.

Serving: You can eat this delicious curry with some brown rice or whole wheat bread.

Nutritional Value Per Serving: *Calories: 448, Carbs: 12 g, Protein: 28 g, Fat: 29 g*

Crockpot Lamb Pasta (Serves 4)

Ingredients:

- 10.5 oz. (300 g) lamb, minced
- One inch (2.5 cm) 3 minced garlic cloves
- 2 medium sized onions, chopped
- 7 oz. (200g) macaroni
- 5 medium sized tomatoes, finely chopped
- 1 teaspoon red chilli flakes
- 3 tablespoons pasta sauce
- ½ teaspoon pepper
- 1 teaspoon salt
- 13.5 fl. oz. (400 ml) vegetable stock
- 2 tablespoons extra virgin olive oil

Method:

1. In a slow cooker, add some olive oil and sauté the garlic and onions in it for 5-6 minutes on medium flame.
2. Add the lamb, chopped tomatoes, pasta sauce, pepper, red chilli flakes, salt, vegetable stock and cook for 6-6.5 hours on low heat. Once done, add salt, uncooked macaroni and cook it for another 25 minutes.

Nutritional Value Per Serving: *Calories: 394, Carbs: 19 g, Protein: 19 g, Fat: 11 g*

Conclusion

It's easier to fall prey to the numerous diet fads that are trending these days. Most of them are scam diets which prove to be of no help when you are trying to lose weight. When you randomly chose a diet for yourself without knowing if will yield the results you want, it will only be a waste of time.

A low-carb diet has been researched by many and has proven to be one of the most effective diet programs to shed excess pounds. All you need to do is consume balanced meals which are low on carbohydrates and consist of proteins, vitamins and minerals.

Along with diet, some light workouts can also accelerate your weight loss. Regardless of the diet program you pick, it should always be combined with some sort of physical activity. You can add your own twist to the recipes mentioned in the book, but try not to deviate too much as these recipes are strategically designed to help you lose weight.

Make it a habit of using fresh ingredients for your dishes for higher nutritional value of the food. Healthy living should be a way of life rather than resorting to occasional diet programs. Let this eBook be a guide on your journey to weight loss.

Recommended Reading for You

You may also want to check my other book:

-> Anti Inflammatory Diet: Beginner's Guide: What You Need To Know To Heal Yourself with Food + Recipes + One Week Diet Plan

"He who takes medicine and neglects to diet wastes the skill of his doctors." -Chinese Proverb

Are you suffering from the severe symptoms that you've been trying to overcome for a long time now using your prescribed pills, but just stuck somewhere in the middle?

Unrestrained inflammation lead to asthma, allergies, tissue and cell degeneration, heart diseases, cancer and various other maladies, which are difficult to deal with.

I myself suffered from long and gruesome periods of acute inflammation. **I had IBS symptoms and very bad, extremely painful sinusitis.** It started to affect my day-to-day ability to work, and my potential and productivity suffered a steep decline. Medication helped, but **the effect was only temporary.** The fact that I was slightly overweight did not help either. I would be confined to my house for days without any solution to my problem. **Every doctor I visited could pinpoint the superficial problem and treat it, time after time, but none could tell me what was causing this problem.**

Vast majority of the recipes I included in this book can be prepared really fast and easily! I also included absolutely delicious One Week Diet Plan for you!

->Direct Buy Link:

http://www.amazon.com/dp/B00MQ9HI58/

->Paperback Version:

https://www.createspace.com/4974692

-> **Fast Freezer Meals: 46 Delicious and Quick Gluten-Free Slow Cooker Recipes for Make-Ahead Meals That Will Save Your Time and Improve Your Health**

Discover Delicious and Quick Gluten-Free Slow Cooker Recipes for Make-Ahead Meals That Will Save Your Time and Improve Your Health!

As a busy businesswoman, wife and mom I know exactly how hard it is to prepare healthy and tasty meals for me and my family every day, especially when they have to be gluten-free! See yourself that gluten-diet doesn't have to be bland, and home cooking doesn't have to be time-consuming!

Most of these recipes can be prepared in no more than 30 minutes and then just effortlessly cooked in your crockpot when you're at work or doing your business!
-I included a shopping list inside to save your precious time.
-No matter if you are gluten intolerant or not – these meals are delicious, healthy and suitable for everyone!
-In this book you will also find freezing and thawing safety guide.
These recipes will enrich your culinary experience and let you save massive time!

->Direct Buy Link: http://www.amazon.com/dp/B00M783PS2/

-> Paperback Version: https://www.createspace.com/4944068

-> Gluten Free Crock Pot Recipes: Healthy, Easy and Delicious Slow Cooker Paleo Recipes for Breakfast, Lunch and Dinner

Discover Healthy, Easy and Delicious Slow Cooker Paleo Recipes for Breakfast, Lunch and Dinner for You and Your Family!

Save your time and start healthy living with these delectable slow cooker gluten free recipes tailor-made for busy people!

I've been on the Gluten Free diet for more than ten years now! Although the main reason for my radical diet change was my diagnosis (Coeliac disease), **I would never-ever (even if given a magical chance) take the lane of eating gluten again.** The Gluten Free diet will help you **detoxify, lose extra weight, minimize catching colds/getting sick too often and feel younger - both mentally and physically.**

->Direct Buy Link: http://www.amazon.com/dp/B00K5UVYUA/

-> Paperback Version: https://www.createspace.com/4823966

-> Gluten-Free Vegan Cookbook: 90+ Healthy, Easy and Delicious Recipes for Vegan Breakfasts, Salads, Soups, Lunches, Dinners and Desserts for Your Well-Being

Discover Healthy, Easy and Delicious Gluten-Free Vegan Recipes for You and Your Family!

Gluten-Free Vegan diet doesn't have to be bland and boring at all! These recipes are original, easy to make and just delightfully appetizing. They will enrich your culinary experience and let you enjoy your breakfasts, lunches, dinners and desserts with your friends and family.

Start living healthy today! I've Included a Shopping List Inside to Save Your Precious Time!

No matter what are your reasons to follow vegan, gluten-free or both of these diets, this book will provide you with many great cooking ideas that me and my family developed during our gluten-free years.

In this book you will find:

-23 Scrumptious and Easy Breakfasts
-27 Delicious and Savory Lunches and Dinners
-22 Aromatic And Nutritious Soups
-21 Enticing And Rich Desserts
-Extra Shopping List to Save Your Precious Time
= 93 Fantastic Gluten-Free Healthy Vegan Recipes!

->Direct Buy Link:
http://www.amazon.com/dp/B00LU915YA/

-> Paperback Version:
https://www.createspace.com/4907669

-> **Paleo Smoothie Recipes: 67 Delicious Paleo Smoothies for Weight Loss and a Healthy Lifestyle – Annette Goodman**

67 Easy and Fast Delicious Smoothie Recipes for Effective Weight Loss and Sexy Body!

Kill the food cravings and get in shape with these delicious and healthy Paleo Smoothies!

In This Book I'll Show You:

-Why Paleo Smoothies are great for Weight Loss (and Weight Maintenance!)
-67 Tasty Paleo Recipes great for Weight Loss, Detox, and keeping your body Healthy every day!
-How to make the Paleo approach easier!
-Important facts about some of the ingredients you'd like to know.
-Planning and Directions – how to get started fast!
-How to maintain your motivation, finally lose the extra pounds and be happy with a Sexy Body!

->Direct Buy Link:
http://www.amazon.com/dp/B00J8ZHMIQ/

-> Paperback Version:
https://www.createspace.com/4803901

My Mailing list: If you would like to **receive new Kindle reads** on **weight loss, wellness, diets, recipes and healthy living** for **FREE** I invite you to my Mailing List. Whenever my new book is out, I set the free period for two days. You will get an e-mail notification and will **be the first to get the book for free** during its limited promotion.

Why would I do this when it took me countless hours to write these e-books?

First of all, that's my way of saying **"thank you"** to my new readers. Second of all – **I want to spread the word about my new books and ideas.** Mind you that **I hate spam and e-mails that come too frequently** - no worries about that.

If you think that's a good idea and are in, just follow this link:

http://eepurl.com/6elQD

You can also follow us on Facebook:

www.facebook.com/HolisticWellnessBooks

We have created this page with a few fellow authors of mine. We hope you find it inspiring and helpful.

Thank You for your time and interest in our work!

Annette Goodman & Holistic Wellness eBooks

About The Author

Hello! My name is Annette Goodman.

I'm glad we met. Who am I?

A homegrown cook, successful wellness aficionado and a writer. I live in Portland, Oregon with my husband, son and our dear golden retriever, Fluffy. I work as a retail manager in of the European companies.

My entire childhood I suffered from obesity, hypertension and complexion problems. During my college years I decided to turn my life around and started my weight-loss and wellness pursue. After more than a decade I can say that I definitely succeeded and now I'd like to give you a hand.

I love creating new healthy recipes, cooking and writing books about healthy lifestyle for you to enjoy and profit from.

I hope we'll meet again!

Author Page on Amazon:

http://www.amazon.com/Annette-Goodman/e/B00LLPE1QM

Made in the USA
Middletown, DE
12 February 2016